T0029338

TO:

FROM:

BUILD GREAT TEAMS

HOW TO HARNESS, CREATE, AND BE PART OF A POWERFUL TEAM

Catherine Hakala-Ausperk

CONTENTS

Introduction   v

▶ **WELCOME TO YOUR TEAM!**   1

Week One: Multigenerational

   Staff   2

Week Two: Graveyard Stew   4

Week Three: The Setting   6

Week Four: The Architect   8

▶ **RECRUITING**   11

Week One: Gaps   12

Week Two: Throwing the Net   14

Week Three: The Hiring Team   16

Week Four: The Right Foot   18

▶ **NARROWING**   21

Week One: First Impressions   22

Week Two: A Book by Its Cover   24

Week Three: Flags   26

Week Four: Setting the Stage   28

▶ **INTERVIEWING**   31

Week One: Answers   32

Week Two: Questions   34

Week Three: The Big Day   36

Week Four: Decision Time   38

▶ **BLENDING**   41

Week One: The Invitation   42

Week Two: The Welcome Mat   44

Week Three: Clarity   46

Week Four: Working with a Net   48

▶ **FOUNDATIONS**   51

Week One: Everything 101   52

Week Two: The Tortoise and

   the Hare   54

Week Three: Catchphrases   56

Week Four: Everyone Has Their

   Own Curve   58

▷ **COMMUNICATION & GROWTH**   **61**

Week One: Your Best Hat   62

Week Two: En Masse   64

Week Three: The Power of

     the Pen   66

Week Four: Unspoken   68

▷ **RESOLUTIONS**   **71**

Week One: Defining Issues   72

Week Two: Coaching Options   74

Week Three: Positive Discipline   76

Week Four: The Final

     Consequences   78

▷ **ACTIONS**   **81**

Week One: Making Decisions   82

Week Two: Understanding

     Viewpoints   84

Week Three: Demystifying

     Delegation   86

Week Four: Building

     Confidence   88

▷ **PLANNING & STRATEGY**   **91**

Week One: Your Defining

     Purpose   92

Week Two: Painless Planning   94

Week Three: Team Planning   96

Week Four: Strategic Careers   98

▷ **TEAM ENVIRONMENT**   **101**

Week One: Winning Culture   102

Week Two: Valuing Values   104

Week Three: Language,

     Legends, Myths, and Reality   106

Week Four: Home Sweet

     Home   108

▷ **INTENTIONAL SUCCESS**   **111**

Week One: Be a New Leader,

     Even If You're Not   112

Week Two: This Time Next

     Year   114

Week Three: What about

     Tomorrow?   116

Week Four: Leading Teams   118

About the Author   *120*

INTRODUCTION

"Can I talk to you for a minute?"

Oh boy. We've all heard that one and grimaced, right? Someone is about to tell you they're quitting. As though your car was creeping ever so slowly up to the tip of the roller coaster and about to slam straight down the other side, reality hits. Your team is about to change!

Arrrggggh! The paperwork! The arguing! Who will do the work in the meantime? What will they say about you in their exit interview? Will you finally get to choose your own person or just take whomever "they" give you? *Arrrggggh! No! I was just getting ready to start making this team work!*

Wake up. You're having a nightmare. It is not, nor should it ever be, this hard to hear the news that someone is leaving your staff. Team development is an ongoing process that should not only withstand periods of change but even celebrate them as opportunities for growth. Right?

If you're not convinced, then this is the book for you!

Set aside some time to go through this book, week by week and hour by hour, and you'll read and practice ideas that will have you not only *prepared* for that next knock on the door but able to wish your departing staff member well and then actually look forward to rebuilding your team even better than before!

MONTH 1

WELCOME TO YOUR TEAM!

MULTIGENERATIONAL STAFF

Most companies today are blessed with multigenerational staff. Within them, you could probably produce both an expert on paper shelf lists and another on iPads. You need to know that. Just imagine the different opinions they might hold toward something you might consider quite innocuous.

Work, rules, expectations, goals, and communication can all change, and they probably should. But people do not. Since teams are made up of people, it's up to the leader—you—to learn and understand that difference. You need to work effectively to define and strengthen culture, outline and articulate achievement, and lead your team to greatness, but first you need to know with whom you're dealing and how to help them get where you're going. Learn about your team's past. Ask questions. Encourage reflection. Review, revisit, and analyze the strengths, weaknesses, opportunities, and threats you find *before* charting a new strategy to move your team forward. Learning all this and considering it carefully will help bring everything about this wonderful resource you get to work with—your team—into focus for you. It's the best first step you can take.

GRAVEYARD STEW

Let's get one thing straight—you do not own your team. They are individuals coming together under your leadership for a temporary period, and you're just privileged to be currently directing their work.

Apart, your team members possess traits and skills that are unique to their training, background, and attitude. Together, they comprise an impressive and potentially effective group of people whose value to your organization is exponentially greater than that of its parts. Under your direction, the impact of that value is limitless.

If you've been fortunate enough to have eaten at the table of a Depression-era friend or family member, you may be familiar with Graveyard Stew. My grandmother, a Finnish immigrant, could turn water into wine after all those years of making do with very little. Anything and everything handy at dinnertime went into the Graveyard Stew pot, and (in spite of its depressing name) what came out was somehow pure heaven. I think of her stew when I think of blending people into outstanding teams.

Think of the goals your team has most recently accomplished and consider your most outstanding employee. Could she or he have accomplished it alone? Doubtful, you have to admit. Your team was a success, and it's up to you to make sure that continues! Certainly now, with your dedication to improvement, it will be, since you have such a diverse and respected staff to work alongside.

THE SETTING

Now it's time to think about where everything happens. What's it like to be where your team works?

At the online retailer Zappos, according to Carmine Gallo, everyone truly loves coming to work. Their CEO outlines five basic reasons for his company's positive culture:

1. Everyone, from customers to employees, is treated like family.

2. They hire for a cultural fit. Without ignoring skills and abilities, supervisors consider personality, friendliness, and passion when selecting new employees.

3. Managers trust their teams. Simple as that sounds, it's too often untrue.

4. Everything is shared. Decisions are open, information is available, and employees are kept in the loop.

5. Staff are encouraged to have fun. The relaxed, supportive atmosphere is a result of the culture and translates into success for the organization.

Take a hard look at the culture in which your employees work before moving forward. If the culture needs to be changed, you can do that. One of the greatest gifts (and requirements) of leadership is to effect change.

THE ARCHITECT

As the architect of your team's future, you're almost ready to begin building, blending, and growing your staff members' skills and ambitions, all while meeting your goals. You're going to get busy. There are going to be more tasks to accomplish than time. Small problems are going to multiply as the pressure of day-to-day survival mounts. The easiest thing to do in reaction is to just start treading water; don't do that.

When you hear yourself saying, "Sure, I'd love to take that course or go to that workshop or attend that conference...but I'm just too busy to get better," remember one other inescapable fact about time: you are in charge of it. If you've never taken a time management course or read a book on the subject, now would be a great time to start. Your time will be limited, your demands will grow, and your priorities, if you're not careful, could slip. There's no shame in relearning how to file, sort, schedule, and juggle your time.

If you want to have a great team, it will need to have a focused, talented, and available leader. The work ahead of you is rewarding at least and life-changing at best. Clear your desk. Get organized. Get ready. Your team, with all its past, present, and future, is waiting.

Lead.

MONTH 2

RECRUITING

GAPS

Every team will lose members from time to time. What should you do first? I'd recommend you get out a piece of paper and number it one through three.

1. Consider what work will not get done once your employee leaves. It's no secret that over the years, some staff members will create enough work to fill their paid hours, whether that work is really key to

the organization's mission or not. Make sure that when the task list you create is complete, it truly reflects a viable position. Don't fill hours; fill work.

 Imagine what tasks you want the person in this position to do that haven't been done before. Now is your chance to build them in as expectations and not just blind hope. Perhaps customer needs have evolved to a point where new programs or services would be appreciated. Now is the perfect time to build them into performance expectations and standards.

3 Think of the personality of the team and what skills a new person should have to make it stronger.

When you've finished this exercise, you will have begun to craft a new perspective on what might just be an outdated job description. You will also have created a personalized gap analysis that will direct the rest of your and your hiring team's decision in how to fill (or not fill) this position.

THROWING THE NET

When you're ready to cast your net, throw it wide and look for people who can enrich, broaden, stretch, and differentiate your team. So how do you attract that variety? Let's talk a bit about the job ad you're about to write.

What's the first rule of advertising your opening? **Don't use the ad your team has always used.** If it truly describes the person you are seeking, then go ahead and get some more mileage out of it.

Once you've written the part of your ad that describes the team and the job, you've got one more decision to make. Other than an application or résumé, what else could you ask for? It has to be something that's going to make a difference in what you know about the applicant!

As long as you ask questions that truly reveal a person's knowledge, skills, abilities, and background, you're going to learn things that will really, truly matter. While some people might characterize these pieces of the package as barriers, I say bring them on!

Now comes the important part. You have envisioned and described the perfect team position you now have the chance to fill. You've written a creative and compelling ad. Now place it where the people you're seeking will find it! There's still more work to do before the responses start coming in, but at least when they do, both you and they will be in the right ballpark.

THE HIRING TEAM

Any day now, all those application materials are going to start flowing into your HR office. But you've still got a lot of work to do before you can begin to sort through all that information. Namely, you have to get your hiring team in place!

Involving other staff members on a hiring team can be almost like teaching a course in teamwork. Think of the elements of blending that you can highlight through this process. You can emphasize existing team members' strengths and weaknesses and recognize openly that it's okay to have both. Together, you can identify the core skills and contributions that will strengthen your team so that once you've found them, an initial level of respect and appreciation will already exist. And perhaps most importantly, you can grow leadership qualities and skills for all involved by coaching them to develop openness, communication, and decision-making skills.

If this sounds like a lot of work, then you're paying attention. It is and should be a considerable process to seek, identify, evaluate, and select a new member of your team. Involve your team and you'll be building foundational synergy that will move you all forward—together.

THE RIGHT FOOT

Since you're in charge of your own hiring story, you can write a better one. The following steps, which have actually been used by organizations for some time, might get your ideal candidate list and your imagination going.

1. Respond immediately to the receipt of an application with a message that doesn't just acknowledge that you got it but conveys excitement.

2. Continue open, formal, or informal communication (depending on your culture) that keeps the applicant apprised of the process and progress.

3. Review the applicant materials quickly and notify the sender if parts are missing. Don't eliminate just yet for such errors, do so later if it is a close call.

4. Describe the interview experience completely ahead of time.

5. Communicate in writing the timeline of your decision-making following the interview.

6. Keep your options open. Don't ever tell a candidate they did not get the job until the one who did get it signs on the dotted line.

7. Emphasize that it's not appropriate for anyone involved in hiring to discuss any part of the process outside the hiring team.

Everyone will be looking to you throughout this process. Communicate openly, be excited, be honest, and put your best foot forward.

MONTH 3

NARROWING

FIRST IMPRESSIONS

After all the careful thought and analysis that's (hopefully) gone into this opportunity to bring in a new team member, the process shouldn't speed up at this point. Instead, it should begin to slow down as you carefully and strategically home in on the perfect new fit. There's a lot more at stake here as you build a great team than just filling another seat at the desk. Let's consider for just a moment the role of Human Relations' staff at this juncture.

Many organizations aren't blessed with large enough staffing budgets to employ trained HR personnel, so administrators fill that role. Others have entire departments dedicated to HR and personnel operations. Both options can work, as long as their contribution to team development remains in support of the team leader's autonomy and not in lieu of it.

Your team is forming first impressions as soon as résumés begin to come in and as soon as you review them together. This is your first look, your first chance to reflect and really listen to one another, and your first opportunity to be as fair as you can be. This process is also logical and replicable; both are considered hallmarks of a professional hiring system. Clearly, without the manpower, time, and energy to personally interview everyone, some discriminating measures must come first. The best ones to use are the ones you've already identified, which happily leaves room for even more surprises down the road, since you're almost ready for the first interview.

A BOOK BY ITS COVER

Whoever originally said you can't judge a book by its cover must have done a lot of interviewing. You need to find a way to look behind the paperwork.

What do you want to know? You've read the cover letters, reviewed the standardized application forms, and perhaps even evaluated written answers to pre-screening tests. Still, do you know all you want to know about each person? If the answer is yes, then you're making progress. But whether the answer is yes or no, think about what else you could learn from either a simple, straightforward prescreening tool or something more elaborate and creative. Maybe you and your team need to take the time to dig a little deeper and strengthen your understanding of the potential team members you are considering.

And there's one more benefit worth mentioning. The prescreening event would also provide you with the opportunity to show your organization's culture, spirit, and even personality to the applicants, so they can eventually make the right decision as well. Both the team and the candidate will have an important decision to make, and the more each knows about the other, the better the outcome is likely to be.

FLAGS

A security expert and former FBI agent once pointed out that every time you see reporters on TV interviewing the neighbors of a recently arrested criminal, they always crack the front door just a bit, peer suspiciously out, and admit they'd always thought there was something weird about that guy! His point? Trust your instincts!

Admittedly, most hiring supervisors get a gut feeling after their very first review of the applicant pool about who is likely to get the job and who isn't. It happens, and especially with very experienced team leaders, there's no avoiding it. Still, those same experienced leaders know that all the other careful steps in the hiring process are critical, and they don't step over them in a rush to take action on their intuition.

Throughout this process though, be sure to pay attention to the flags you sometimes see waving at you during these structured, analytical steps. Those flags need to be recognized and the information they represent brought into consideration. When you are truly intent on building a great team, you will slow down and let the flags do their job—to make you think, maybe beyond what you can even see or prove.

It's a delicate dance. Team leaders have to listen to their own opinions and reactions without ignoring contrary thoughts from their teams while also watching for subtle flags and keeping all these elements in objective balance.

SETTING THE STAGE

It's almost interview time. For days now (or longer), you've been wrapped up in reviewing paperwork, scoring qualifications, and rating applicants. At this point, you might want to push the paperwork away for a short time and refocus on the team you already have working for you.

On an ongoing basis, you should have been providing continual feedback on the skills, accomplishments, and goals of each member of your team. Now is a great time to meet with each person and reexamine your shared mission, recognize their contribution to it, and assure them that their opportunities for continued success will be enhanced—and not threatened—by the new person you'll be bringing on board. Further, by emphasizing the critical role they will all play in the new person's success, you could outline as a group the induction procedures and processes planned for your new hire. By the time that person arrives on her first morning, everyone on your team should have a role to play in the orientation, which can cement not only the new person's sense of belonging but also the individual value each person feels toward their own place in the group.

Ask for ideas. Design your new employee's first week as a group. Let your team tell you what's important for success, and together you can find ways to impart that knowledge to the new person. Investing in the success of a new team member—and the future success of the team overall—needs to be a shared objective.

INTERVIEWING

ANSWERS

As clichéd as it might sound, you'll never know if you've arrived at your destination if you don't know where you're going to begin with. Most traditional interview questions are proficient at leading you down that proverbial path. This often happens because interviewers don't begin their questions by considering what they are hoping to hear! More often than not, they just pull an old interview out of the drawer, blow the dust off, and dive right in.

Tell me about your background. Yawn!

Instead, you could try opening with "What's the coolest thing you've gotten to do lately?" It's relaxed, it's fun, and you'll learn what they think of as an accomplishment, what really gets them energized, and whether the work they most enjoy is a realistic match for your current opening.

You'll know quite a bit about your interviewees by the time they've been selected. The interview itself should tell you what *else* you need to learn. Résumés and applications give you the nuts and bolts of a person professionally. What's missing? Make a list of what you don't know, either from inconsistencies or omissions in their application, and then formulate questions that will address those points.

This is your team that's developing. Rare is the opportunity to enhance it, grow it, and prepare it for a strong and successful future. What do you REALLY need to know about that perfect person?

QUESTIONS

When designing questions, your number one goal should be to learn something new. Try using some of these ideas as inspiration.

▶ **Ask how.** Including *how* in any question can open it up far enough that your candidate has a chance to really share a part of themselves.

▶ **Make them convince you.** Use your hiring team as

guinea pigs and watch the different answers you can get by asking variations of the same question.

▶ **Get their own words.** Instead of "Why should we hire you for this job?" try "When the other candidates call me and ask why we picked you, what should I tell them?"

▶ **Ask for examples.** Asking "Can you give us a couple of examples that demonstrate that?" takes them beyond that simplicity to really delve into the truth.

▶ **Ask what if?** After a perfect answer to a tough question, throw them for a loop and see if you can figure out what their plan B would be.

▶ **Use silence.** Know when to stop talking. Sometimes it's best to ask it and then sit back and be quiet and let the silence be filled with their comments, not yours. Listen.

▶ **Use real life.** Scenario questions provide an opportunity to let the applicant know what your job is really like and how they'd respond to them.

THE BIG DAY

Your goal in any interview is to put the applicant so at ease that you can learn as much about them as possible and they about you. Unavoidable nervousness can be reduced by a comfortable setting, friendly surroundings, and a generally welcoming environment. Together with your team, think about how you can provide all of those elements, from making sure someone's watching for the applicant and welcoming them by name to barring cell phones and other distractions from the interview room!

Remember, the applicants are interviewing you, too!

Interview day is a special time for everyone involved. It is the culminating opportunity to grow and enhance your team, making your organization and the service you offer more valuable to your stakeholders. Prepare for it. Handle it well. Get everything you can out of it. After all the candidates go home, you and your hiring team will be left with a difficult decision to make, and you're going to want to have collected the best and most information possible to make it well.

DECISION TIME

After all the interviews are completed, it is time to make a decision. Author Harold Messmer Jr. suggests following these guiding principles:

- **Anchor yourself to the hiring criteria.** They should serve as your guiding force in evaluation.
- **Take your time.**
- **Cross-verify.** Always, always, always check references,

even when it seems obvious you shouldn't have to.

▶ **Don't force the issue.** The recruiting process sometimes uncovers a "dream" employee—except for one problem: the candidate's skills and attributes don't match the hiring criteria for the job. Remember the first rule—anchor yourself to the hiring criteria! Don't try to put a "good" employee in the wrong job.

A student once shared with me the single most useful thing she learned from an entire semester class on management. When you have to make a decision, her instructor said, it doesn't matter if you make a good decision or a bad decision. Just make a damn decision!

MONTH 5

BLENDING

THE INVITATION

At this point in your team-building process, when you're almost ready to extend an offer and make someone very, very happy, consider a few factors before moving into the invitation:

▶ **Don't settle.** Picture the candidate's arrival on that first day, and consider your gut feeling. If it's excited anticipation, then move on. If it's prayer, then consider that dreaded *R* word—repost!

▸ **Refold the flags.** In reviewing the interview answers just one more time, was there something the candidate said that you haven't been able to get out of your mind? Get it answered. There's no rule precluding a follow-up phone call just to be sure.

▸ **Check back in with your team.** While you don't have to reach consensus on this major decision, you should want to come as close as possible to that goal as you can.

Each and every step you take in this process furthers your overall goal of building a great team, so they should be considered and implemented with deliberate thought and high integrity. It's time to roll out the welcome mat and get back to work!

THE WELCOME MAT

During the first year on most jobs, many leaders spend what I consider to be an inordinate and unnecessary amount of time apologizing for and fixing mistakes that could have easily been avoided if they'd stuck a little bit closer to the new guy for a bit longer in the beginning.

So should you.

And you can start by considering Richard Rubin's list of where, when, why, who, and how.

▶ **Where:** Go and sit in the work space your new employee will be using. Could you work there?

▶ **When:** Well before an offer is made, you should have a candid discussion with the applicant clarifying schedule expectations. After offer acceptance is not the time to learn they won't work weekends.

▶ **Why:** Without the ability to refer to an approved, standardized personnel manual as a resource, serious credibility issues will undoubtedly surround the validity of any rules you choose to describe.

▶ **Who:** Take proactive, strategic steps to ensure your new team member's introduction to your team is effective, nonthreatening, and enlightened.

▶ **How:** Teams that succeed do so because of an even and shared respect for one another. One way to achieve this level playing field is to establish ground rules early in the game. While direction from the team leader can be useful, the rules must be created and agreed to by the entire team.

CLARITY

No surprises! From the very beginning of their career with you, team members must know, clearly and completely, what will be expected of them in a position. If you don't help them from that very first day, the odds against their and your success increase.

The time is now, on your new team member's first day at work, for just the two of you to sit down and talk. There will be plenty of time in the coming days for team assimilation. Now, it's just between the two of you. It's time to clarify expectations—all of them.

So hit the high points—and the challenging ones—early on. A foundation of honest, open, personal communication can only result in a future built on openness, support, and clarity.

The next logical step on the road to success rests in the achievement of goals and objectives. Since you should be planning at least three evaluations during your new employee's first ninety days, let him take baby steps toward success. Identify one or two goals, and then examine the results together and celebrate achievement. Following a reasonable orientation period, work together to set annual goals and keep those channels of communication open. Don't wait thirty days to sit down and talk. Remember, this is a person in whom you're investing. A lot of time and energy has gone into his arrival at your door. Make him glad he came in.

WORKING WITH A NET

Mentors can make all the difference in the world to your green, nervous, and hopeful new team member. Using mentors isn't the complicated, expensive, and time-consuming experience many believe it to be.

This step, often overlooked and undervalued, can make that first foray inside the door and into the group much easier and much more likely to succeed. That is, after all, your goal. As team leader, you must remain focused on doing whatever you can to ensure that each and every person you supervise will succeed.

The number one thing most employees say they want is interesting work. Next comes appreciation and having a feeling of being included. Imagine how much an established and respected team member can help in those early and important achievements. Valuable, effective, and meaningful mentoring can take place anywhere between a couple of cups of coffee to thirty years of weekly lunches, and everyone will grow in the process—the new employee, the mentor, and most important, your team!

It's almost time to set that valuable new hire of yours free to move into your shared future. Use your team to help ensure a happy ending. Assign a mentor.

FOUNDATIONS

EVERYTHING 101

The honeymoon period with your new employees never really lasts as long as you hope it will, does it? Often, when orienting a new hire, bosses find themselves cutting short their good intentions and getting their new person right into work.

Don't worry. It's never too late. Never. It's time to build a solid foundation upon which the rest of your team development can grow.

New employees need more than a security code to get in the door before opening time; they need to learn the basics of what your organization stands for. Think customer service, the reference interview, telephone etiquette, and the like. And it's up to you to ensure your new team member gets that—no matter how much the place starts falling down around you.

I try to plan my orientation by putting those categories in order and not skipping over number one. Just as you would when you create a strategic plan for your overall organization, the training plan that you and your new hire outline should be clear, measurable, achievable, and somewhat challenging and exciting! As they move through the rest of their learning and development, all their accomplishments and growth should be acknowledged, recognized, and celebrated. You've likely got a long working relationship ahead of you. Lay the foundation, clarify the future, and move into it confidently together.

Build your team right. Start with a plan—and stick to it.

THE TORTOISE AND THE HARE

There's a lot to learn for team members who are seeking success and achievement. Whether they're the new guy in town, like your brand-new hire, or the longtime specialists who know their roles backward and forward, development never stops. Or at least it shouldn't.

As the team leader, one of your biggest challenges is to get your team to understand and come to terms with this expectation without feeling overwhelmed and helpless in the face of an unachievable goal. Enter the tortoise and the hare—slow and steady wins the race. No one expects you or them to skyrocket to the top, breaking records and establishing new paradigms along the way. What is expected, or at least should be, is that you can create a culture of continual growth and improvement, both individually and then collectively, that will support a never-ending expansion of value to the organization.

Any decent book on team building has to take an occasional jog away from focusing on the team members and bring the spotlight back to you—the team leader—and your role in keeping the ship afloat. You can do that with a steady, unwavering commitment to excellence that can't be jarred by staff changes, budget cuts, or technological advances. Continual development and growth isn't just for the team—it's for you, too!

That model is your team's ticket to success.

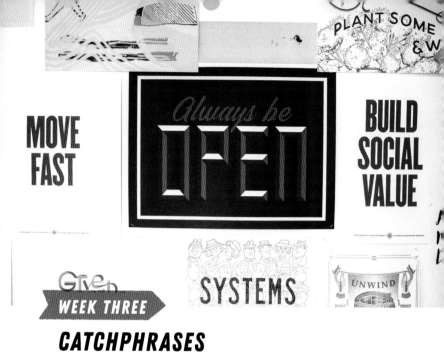

CATCHPHRASES

Catchphrases are fun, aren't they? A quick and dirty internet search turns up examples such as "Git 'r done!" "Yada, yada, yada," and my personal favorite, "He's dead, Jim" (from *Star Trek*). Recently, in the world of management and team building, a new favorite catchphrase is "learning organization." What's that about?

This section of *Build Great Teams* has a distinct purpose. That is to convince you, against all odds and against great temptation, to remain committed wholly to creating a true learning organization for your team. Everything else that you'll learn and do in your quest to build a great team will rest entirely on development, growth, and success. There is no such thing as a status quo of excellence.

The next time you get too busy or too stressed or too distracted to stay focused on every team member's right to thrive in a learning environment, consider why taking more care with your team is worth it.

A learning organization provides for superior performance, competitive advantage, great customer relations, improved quality, an understanding of risks, an appreciation of diversity, a commitment to innovation, personal and spiritual well-being, an increased ability to manage change, greater understanding, an energized workforce, expanded boundaries, an engaged internal community, and a sharper awareness and mastery of what the times demand.

Sounds like a lot more than a catchphrase to me.

EVERYONE HAS THEIR OWN CURVE

Picture a bell curve, and you'll get an idea of how your team members will vary in their attitudes toward training and development. Some will be amped up! Others...not so much.

This week's focus is on those team members we've all known or supervised, or maybe even been, who live at the far end of the curve and aren't interested in any training or development, thank you very much. These are the ones who say "just give me my paycheck and I'll do my job."

You owe it to your other team members, your organization, and even these reluctant people to find a way for them to grow at least alongside, if not at the same pace, as the others in your group.

You're trying to establish and perpetuate a true learning organization. Before you get there, you'll need to establish this expectation of accountability. Once training goals and expectations are in place, who should find the workshops or classes? They should. Who should initiate requests for necessary schedule modifications? They should. And who should speak up when knowledge gaps develop? Right. They should.

Make sure your team knows they are invested in the game and that the investment is in their own future. The options they face are really quite clear: adapt or fail. To pretend otherwise is to lead your team down a path to obsolescence.

COMMUNICATION
& GROWTH

YOUR BEST HAT

Here's what your average team leader's to-do list might include: budgeting, scheduling, interviewing, paperwork, filing, and organizing. And here's what each and every one of these interactions *will* include—teaching and coaching. As the leader of your great team, this is not just another hat you will wear but one you will never take off. So you'd better be sure you understand the importance of this role and how best to put it into action.

For the next four weeks, you'll be focusing on the challenges and rewards of teaching and coaching your team. Depending on the task at hand, you'll be providing this important support service in many different ways—person-to-person, in groups of all sizes, through the written word, and by unspoken actions and implications. Because individual learning is always your ultimate goal, start by asking yourself how you could possibly develop a truly great team if you didn't address all your team members' needs, starting with getting to know them one-on-one.

Maybe you've never been a teacher and you're not comfortable with this responsibility. It's really no more complicated than demonstrating that each team member's achievements and challenges are your own as the team's leader. You may be relieved to hear there is no wrong way to coach for success. The only thing you can do wrong is to not take the time to do it. So keep your hat on...and coach!

WEEK TWO

EN MASSE

On his way out the door on my first day and his last, a former boss offered this bit of parting advice: "Be prepared to be met to death." Boy, was he right. These en masse gatherings—called meetings—can offer you a unique and invaluable opportunity to strengthen ties, build trust, and develop loyalties. First, though, you have to learn to master the meeting, using these seven tips from Jason B. Jones:

1. Be on time. Start on time. End on time.

2. Prepare for the meeting. Then over-prepare.

3. Send any support materials along with the (timed) agenda at least a week before the meeting, and create a culture of expected participation.

4. Don't start a meeting unless you know how and when it will end.

5. Meetings are for decisions and distribution of tasks, not for reports. Don't read to attendees.

6. Have a competent chair and rotate the assignment.

7. Share leadership or shift it month to month. Provide training on agenda preparation, facilitation, and any other skills needed for success.

Why bring team members together? All too often, it's simply because it's meeting time. That shouldn't be the answer. Produce a better solution together than would have been possible alone.

THE POWER OF THE PEN

It's time to hone your writing skills. For many staff members whose schedules (or titles) keep them apart from your organization's decision makers, you're the translator. When you write well, they can understand more clearly, and their motivation, confidence, and performance will improve.

Consider these four important implications, suggested by Karl Walinskas.

1. Your writing will have a visible impact. Seeing something in writing makes it more believable and increases recall. It can also provide invaluable legal support.

2. It's been said that unless you have a plan written down, you don't have a plan. Written messages can better avoid being manipulated and twisted throughout the chain of command, whether intentionally or unintentionally.

3. Concerns, complaints, and requirements can go through several steps before they reach the person who can respond to them, often resulting in the old telephone-game confusion. Recorded requests can comfortably make that trip.

4. When praise is received in private over a cup of coffee, it's nice. When it's posted in black and white in the newsletter—in writing—it's like giving someone an unexpected bonus.

UNSPOKEN

Pssst. Guess what I just heard?

Speaking and writing aren't the only ways messages get sent in a team. Messages, often the wrong ones, have a way of sending themselves. And that is something else critical for team leaders to consider—and avoid!

First on this list of alternative communications is things that team members see, hear, feel, and know (or think they know) that you never meant to convey. Let's start with what they hear, such as gossip.

Gossip is a no-win situation. People are hurt, time is wasted, information gets convoluted, and—worse—customers are left waiting. Allow no time or acceptance of gossip on your team, and keep your communication and theirs aboveboard, healthy, and transparent.

As the team leader, the best way you can combat indirect, inaccurate, and unproductive communication is to battle it with the direct stuff, so get comfortable communicating—any way you can—to your team. Invite thoughtful, constructive commentary. Encourage double-checking and fact-seeking in place of wondering, or worse, guessing, and above all, make kindness toward one's teammates every person's paramount goal. As we learned as children, healthy teams must always think before they speak.

MONTH 8

RESOLUTIONS

DEFINING ISSUES

Wherever there are people, there will be conflicts, contrasts, challenges, and disruption of all kinds. Since you are the person they'll turn to for help, this month's lessons focus on resolution. Conflict resolution is really just another way to grow and develop that diverse and rich group of people you call a team.

Still, before you can bring them together, it helps to be able to understand them apart. If you haven't yet led your team through a personality assessment event, such as the Myers-Briggs Type Indicator or the Riso-Hudson Enneagram Type Indicator, it's time you did. There is immeasurable value in helping diverse people get to know one another better and, as a result, come to understand one another.

After you've gotten to know your team members better, it will be easier for you to then hear (and understand) everyone's version of events, then get them working to resolve the real problem at hand. There are more steps you can and should take so that everyone involved learns and grows from conflict experience. First, document the problem, then look for obstacles, not excuses, and finally plan a way together to remove them before someone stumbles over them again. Convey your confidence in your team, find a way to subtly congratulate them on the growth all experienced, and plan for improvement.

COACHING OPTIONS

Now that you know the whole story, what's next? The problem is still out there. Emotions are still running high, feelings are still being hurt, and the health of your team overall is at stake. This is when you become a coach.

Coaching is different from training. It's more holistic, for one thing. For another, it's more personal (professionally personal, not personal personal), and it requires more investment from both parties. Why should a member of your team want to invest energy and effort in working with you as a coach? Because we're all in this together.

In times of celebration and in times of conflict, you—as the coach—need to continually remind and demonstrate to your team that resolution is everyone's job. And sometimes coaching is the best way to support that work. Good, effective coaching has no beginning and no end. Coaching isn't limited to a special task or assignment. It is a perpetual learning relationship that results in more than just resolution—it results in growth. Coaching is more important than being right; it's about making the situation right.

Sometimes it's harder to help someone out of a jam than at other times. If you're coaching your team out of a difficult, contentious situation and you've started by collecting all the facts and hearing all sides of the story, move forward carefully. What comes next is finding a healing, positive way to repair damage and move forward stronger.

POSITIVE DISCIPLINE

Most organizations have disciplinary charts or policies, and they have them for a reason. Once all other options have been exhausted and a problem remains, discipline remains the clear, appropriate choice. What's important now is that it should be handled professionally, impersonally, and effectively. If you don't have established steps to follow, it might be time to write some. Discipline policies provide a support system for leaders and employees alike, so both can be certain decisions and actions taken are reasonable, predetermined (not knee-jerk), and appropriate. The team leader, by the time of the first disciplinary meeting, should have finished doing her or his homework and should have all the facts of the incident or issue under scrutiny at hand. Now is the time to review the facts objectively, then clarify the problem.

When looking for solutions, always include hope. This is the team leader's best tool to use to demonstrate that all is not lost. There's a correction available to get the individual back on track. Be clear. Be specific. You're going to have to reevaluate for progress down the road, so don't be nebulous in your expectations for improvement.

THE FINAL CONSEQUENCES

While it's true that no one likes to talk about firing people, you can't fix everything. Although traumatic for all involved, experienced leaders will often comment after a termination that they wished they'd done it sooner! Consider these alternatives to finding a lasting solution:

▶ **Morale:** Other team members wonder why they're

working so hard when the person next to them is playing online games and nothing is ever done.

▶ **Motivation:** Team members wonder why they should take on more work when they're already doing their part *and* carrying someone else's share.

▶ **Productivity:** If other team members, no matter how dedicated, simply cannot pick up the slack for poor performers, then something isn't getting done.

▶ **Reputation:** An organization's reputation with its clientele is only as good as the worst interaction they've had. Once you allow a poor employee to send someone away mad, guess what? They probably won't be back.

▶ **Integrity:** Once a team leader has let one person slide because they can't face the uncomfortable option of firing, it won't be long before they dodge the next big issue before them as well. And the next. Eventually, trains without conductors derail.

MONTH 9

ACTIONS

MAKING DECISIONS

If you've been a member of a team at any point, you've undoubtedly experienced being dragged through a lengthy decision-making process only to learn that the final decision was really a foregone conclusion. Why were you asked to contribute in the first place then? Good question. Approached correctly, well-managed decision-making can reduce the resentments built from false involvement while also building an honest, trusting relationship. Plus, decisions can actually get made too!

Faced with a needed decision, start by considering how it should be made and by whom. Clearly, some decisions must be handled at the executive or team leadership level. For reasons ranging from confidentiality to legality and beyond, leaders can't and shouldn't involve team members in deciding issues that could result in conflict. You wouldn't ask the team to decide which of three coworkers should be laid off. For issues that require team input, a variety of opinions, and a diversity of insight, however, the team should be invited to participate. While leaders will sometimes need to set parameters, on other occasions, options can be left wide open.

UNDERSTANDING VIEWPOINTS

There's one other major factor that individuals uncon-
sciously bring to the team table that you, as the team
leader, need to understand and blend into your shared
success, and that is a generational background and
the unique characteristics and work habits associated
with it. While it would be foolhardy and inaccurate to
say these qualities apply evenly to each and every individual, they've still been upheld by enough repeated

studies to demonstrate a real and important impact on the workplace. Today's workforce has been categorized by sociologists into several major categories of impact. Paraphrasing Carrie Ballone and, okay, throwing in a little stereotyping, here are some strengths just a few of your teammates might be contributing already:

▶ **1946–1964: Baby boomers.** People from this generation are optimistic and rule challengers. Support their career development and show them that both their status and impact can continue to increase.

▶ **1965–1980: Generation X.** These people are self-reliant and technologically engaged. Communicate to them what a great impact the team's successful reaching of organizational goals will have on them.

▶ **1981–1996: Generation Y.** Also known as millennials, people born in this generation are achievement oriented and technology driven. They care about the social and environmental issues surrounding everything and want to find a way to contribute.

DEMYSTIFYING DELEGATION

Easy as delegation may sound, it requires strategy, knowledge of your team, and a dedication to both their and your organization's overall success. Do you see opportunities for delegation and a more effective distribution of workload here? What if, in order to increase everyone's commitment and contribution, you worked together to loosen the distinctions and divisions under long-held job descriptions and allowed for flexibility to share assignments? The trust demonstrated by the manager would not only build pride and skill throughout the team, it would also free up more of her time for developing the group in other ways. That's using the power of delegation for good instead of evil.

Humans learn from making mistakes—and then correcting them. When an employee is shut out of the correction process, humiliated by failure, and frustrated by lost opportunities to shine, what else could we expect to result but belittled, unappreciated, and undervalued people whose allegiance to the team grows weaker by the day?

Share the work and give away the praise. Support the work by keeping tabs on progress and addressing speed bumps. Leadership and follow-up, when done right, are called development. When done wrong, they're called micromanagement. Don't avoid the former to escape the latter.

BUILDING CONFIDENCE

Even in the most well-balanced, diverse teams, there can remain one major stumbling block that can replace action with inaction (at best) and antipathy (at worst.) That roadblock is confidence, or the lack thereof. Few leaders possess or demonstrate the confidence to fail. But that can be fixed.

First, remove fear, both theirs and yours. What are you afraid of? Usually, it's as simple as failure, but it can be as complicated as embarrassment, loss of respect, or just plain being wrong.

One of the strongest actions you can take to reduce fear and build confidence is to put yourself and your own weaknesses out there for everyone to see, and, while they're watching, show them the corrections as well. If the boss can fail, repair damage, and move on, then everyone can!

Next, build passion. Little strengthens a sense of camaraderie more than a shared passion or zeal for goals. Staff who believe that coworkers share their dedication are more confident in stepping up their game due to the shared commitment they all feel.

Finally, seize opportunities. If you raise your hand first, going out on a limb to excel, chances are your confident team will be right behind you.

MONTH 10

PLANNING & STRATEGY

YOUR DEFINING PURPOSE

Most people don't trust, value, or certainly look forward to strategic planning. Given the opportunity to take part in planning, they'd probably prefer to go get those long-avoided root canals. Good leaders can change that impression. Good team leaders **must** change that impression. Why? Because in the words of the great Yogi Berra, "If you don't know where you're going, you'll wind up somewhere else." You have embarked on a journey to take your team to greatness. Tell me, how will you know when you've made it?

For many team leaders, opportunities to have a direct impact on their organization's strategic planning process do not abound. Great leaders should change that too. Volunteer to take part so that from the outset of the process, you can develop a clear and motivating understanding of and belief in your team's purpose and goals, and then you can return to your team and get them on that same path to success. Throughout this coming month, team leaders will learn how to truly focus the varied skills, energies, viewpoints, and contributions of their team members into specific actions that contribute to overall success. There's no other place to start this journey than with a strong, clear organizational (or at least team) strategic plan. Lose the excuses and share a purpose.

PAINLESS PLANNING

Picture this. Two football teams, one in red uniforms and one in green, pour out of their respective tunnels and onto the sidelines. They gather in a huddle, jumping up and down to get their blood boiling, then the whistle blows. They all rush onto the field at once, charging at one another, running up and down while wondering, where's the ball?

If you consider the organizational design of a

football team, you've got the owner at the top, then a head coach, then team coaches (defense, offense, special, you get the picture), then the individual players. Clearly, the strategy described above isn't going to get them very far toward their goals. But wait a minute; they don't have any goals yet. No wonder the teams will fail. Just like the individuals you supervise, every person on a team wants to be successful at what they do. They may understand the overall mission (to present the best athletic performance and spectacle), and they may buy in to the team's vision (to be the most sought-after ticket in the league), and they may even share the values of athleticism, sportsmanship, and power, but they're still lacking the framework that will get them there.

Sound strategy begins with established, articulated goals. Before your team can become great, it needs to fully grasp what the goals are and what their particular role is in achieving them. That's success.

TEAM PLANNING

It's time for team leaders to step up to the plate. Your board has set the direction by identifying your goals for the coming year or two. Now, it's up to you to chart your team members' success in attaining those goals. In the planning process, the next step—and your next assignment—is to work with the leadership team to identify measurable objectives.

Objectives should be two things at a minimum.

First, they must be actionable, meaning they should state what will happen in action terms, not philosophical ones. Second, they should be SMART (specific, measurable, attainable, realistic, and time-bound). Objectives can be created using a painless, three-step process. Remember, we started by having the ultimate governing group (board or owners) identify what is to be accomplished. Managers, who know the operation, the staff, and the true potentials, now work to identify how success will happen. Just remember that the number one requirement for that success is your team!

STRATEGIC CAREERS

If you're lucky and you're working in an intentional environment, your organization has already outlined overarching guidelines of mission, vision, values, and planning for you to implement. If it hasn't, you now know how to create these invaluable guideposts for your team. Do that first. Because next, it's time for you to help develop real performance goals for each and every member of your team.

I don't know why, but even outstanding employees always seem to dread that annual evaluation appointment with the boss. Maybe it's because not all leaders adhere to the restriction that evaluations should never contain surprises, so they're expecting to be caught off guard by something awful. Or maybe it's an aversion to the last part of the meeting, because that's when the employee and supervisor should be setting goals for the coming year. What's not clear is whether those goals are dreaded because of the challenge or the futility they represent. If it's the latter, what a shame. And what a lost opportunity for team leaders.

Remember that what most people want from their jobs is an opportunity to matter, to make a contribution, to make a difference. It's up to you to fit your team into your plan so that they can achieve success!

MONTH 11

TEAM ENVIRONMENT

WINNING CULTURE

Because we are, after all, part of the animal kingdom, it's not unfair to begin a discussion about team culture with an analogy to puppies. They're adorable. Climbing all over one another in the puppy crate, each animal has started life with exuberance and an openness to learning. Two of them end up going to different homes. For one, the atmosphere is quiet, serene, and peaceful. Raised by some pretty nice DINKs (double income, no kids), they know when they'll eat, go out, get attention, and rest. Life is orderly and predictable. For the other, chaos abounds. Six kids, keeping all hours, music blaring. Sometimes they eat. Sometimes the Little League games take precedence and dinner is forgotten. Fear, uncertainty, and distrust become the watchwords of the day.

Like those puppies, your team members will be affected by the environment—or culture—that you create, influence, and manage.

Let's keep it simple. Culture is *what's considered normal.* People consider something to be normal if it reflects what they see happen, hear about, and come to believe.

Culture controls how you feel at work. Comfortable? Challenged? Supported? Scared? Clumsy? Unappreciated? Underutilized? Frustrated? Angry? As the team leader, it probably isn't hard to pick the words out of that list that you want your team to feel.

VALUING VALUES

Everything has changed around here! I can't keep up these days; everything is different! These comments often reflect a sense of panic, chaos, and uncertainty that can derail even the most strategic team plan for success.

Here's a simplistic comparison to consider. In a happy, healthy marriage, the two people involved likely start out sharing critical values. Loyalty, love, support, caring, and strength might be included in that list. Fast-forward through about twenty years and consider the changes they might experience. Deaths of friends and parents, financial crises, housing emergencies, layoffs, new jobs, lost jobs, and frightening medical diagnoses are just a few possibilities. How in the world could they weather those changes and remain strong? You guessed it. By relying on their loyalty, love, support, caring, and strength. By relying on their values!

When you're faced with a lot to consider, such as the articulation of a concept as critical as values from an organizational, group, individual, and management perspective, sometimes the view can get cloudy. Strictly from the point of view of team leadership, two values stand out as arguably the most critical to promote: trust and integrity. With these two understood by your team and demonstrated relentlessly by actions, your group's stability will be enhanced beyond measure.

Knowing that what's important won't change will help your team adjust to whatever does.

LANGUAGE, LEGENDS, MYTHS, AND REALITY

Legends always remind me of playing telephone, because as the years go by, they resemble less and less the actual person credited with so strongly impacting the culture. Whether they're pictured as heroes or villains (depending on who tells the story), folklore surrounding their achievements, disasters, or antics can guide, predict, and prevent more progress than the individual themselves ever could. If you're considering attempting to discredit old legends, save your breath.

When team members do something significant that supports your newly realized value system, reward them, celebrate them, and give their achievements a place in the new legends of your culture.

Communication is your best tool here. In attempting to recreate a mythless culture (otherwise known as honest), connect with your team routinely through forums and other avenues in which questions or rumors can be openly addressed. Openly inquire, at every opportunity, "What are you hearing? Are there any questions or crazy answers out there that we can dispel?" By showing your willingness to hear—and respond honestly—to such early myth building, you might just be starting your own, current-day legend of the team leader who really cared what everyone thought.

HOME SWEET HOME

For a lot of team leaders, time spent concentrating on the more serious, service-related issues leaves little time left over for something as innocuous as a messy desk. With that approach as a guide, before you can say "I know it's here somewhere," the team's entire environment can look like your teenage son's bedroom. If you're still thinking, "So what? I have more important things to think about," consider this. With your team starting out on its quest for greatness, which do you think will move them along faster—organized, supportive, inspiring, and comfortable spaces to call their own or dusty, chaotic, uncomfortable, and unwelcoming ones? Don't ignore the effect of the trappings of environment on your team's culture, and don't be afraid to start making changes right now. Unlike arguing with that teenager, improvements won't be as difficult to negotiate or to see put into action.

By now, you should be sold. While much that affects your team's culture is too ephemeral to actually touch, here's something that isn't. Here's a chance to show them their value and your respect for it.

MONTH 12

INTENTIONAL SUCCESS

BE A NEW LEADER, EVEN IF YOU'RE NOT

In this final month of the book, you'll get some tips on how to sort through all these roles and challenges and focus on the right parts at the right times.

This final month of the book will give you a chance to catch your breath and set some priorities. One thing's for sure: You can't do everything you've been reading about all at once. You can't even do most of it every single day. But you can move consistently forward and develop your team's success intentionally, passionately, and decisively. And you can succeed! We'll start with some generalities first, then move on to some more specific actions you can take to chart long- and short-term achievements. Shared in a post on teamworkandleadership.com, these five steps can prepare you well for everything that will come after them.

1. Recognize that you are not alone!
2. Keep the end in mind, and practice patience—daily.
3. Consider setbacks as opportunities.
4. Persevere with confidence.
5. Keep learning.

Realize first that you need to set some clear goals for yourself. One, I hope, will be to continue your commitment to developing your skills as a leader.

THIS TIME NEXT YEAR

Usually, somewhere in one's fifties, the value of having short- and long-term goals becomes glaringly apparent. Okay, so we can't dance till dawn, eat anything and everything we're offered, and worry about money tomorrow. Life begins to clarify the reality that it's time to set some goals. Long term—maybe it's time to concentrate on getting healthy. Short term— not smoking and a little exercise probably wouldn't hurt. There's a professional parallel to this kind of thinking.

For the positive, motivational purposes of your first step in team greatness, use this tool to keep your and your team members' focus sharp. Great evaluations involve analyzing, questioning, listening, and planning. If there are poor performance issues or opportunities to grow, handle them effectively, efficiently, and without rancor. Focus on the future. Focus on your plan for greatness. Plan long and short terms goals to bring your team to greatness in alignment with your shared team and company vision.

WHAT ABOUT TOMORROW?

Before I left a position where I'd worked with the best manager I've ever known (still, to date), she gave me some advice. She told me to give my team something they wanted—and do it early. I'd be in a honeymoon period, she explained, and should take advantage of that period to make some quick decisions and take actions that would give them each something they've longed for. More valuable than words, she said, these decisive actions would demonstrate to them that I was listening, that I would follow up on promises, and most of all, that I cared about their concerns. Now that made sense!

According to Carl Robinson, there are six frequent reasons for turnover. Think each day about how each of these can be avoided:

1. People leave because the work or workplace was not as expected.

2. People leave because of a mismatch between the job and the person.

3. People leave because of too little coaching or feedback.

4. People leave because of too few growth and advancement opportunities.

5. People leave because they feel devalued and unrecognized.

6. People leave because of a loss of trust and confidence in leaders.

LEADING TEAMS

It's time to talk about you.

As the saying goes, "The journey of a thousand miles begins with one step."

If you think of your career as a leader as your professional journey, the beauty of every new day is that you can start that journey over whenever you choose. After this past year's focus on leading your team to greatness, the moment you close this book, you can take another first step, and that is leading your own career toward success. If you remain committed to your own growth and development, there aren't enough detours, pitfalls, or orange barrels in the world to keep you from your goals. Give yourself time. Imagine how many steps it would really take to walk all around the world!

What are you going to read next?

ABOUT THE AUTHOR

Catherine Hakala-Ausperk is an author, speaker, and trainer with over thirty-five years of library experience, in everything from direct customer service to library management and administration. She is an Adjunct Instructor at the iSchool at Kent State and also teaches for the American Library Association's Certified Public Library Administrator (CPLA) Program, the Public Library Association, ALA's eLearning Solutions, the Urban Library Council, InfoPeople, and multiple other organizations. An active speaker, planner, and trainer in libraries across the country, she is the author of seven books: *Be a Great Boss: One Year to Success*

(ALA, 2011); *Build a Great Team: One Year to Success* (ALA, 2013); *Renew Yourself: A Six-Step Plan for More Meaningful Work* (ALA, 2017); and a unique series of leadership planners, including *Future-Proof Your Team*, *Win 'Em Over*, *Dynamic Discipline*, and *Hot Ticket Meetings*. Catherine's passion is for supporting, coaching, and developing great libraries, successful teams, and—especially—strong and effective leaders.

You can learn more about her at librariesthrive.com and like and follow her on Facebook at facebook.com/librariesthrive.

NEW! Only from Simple Truths®

IGNITE READS
spark impact in just one hour

IGNITE READS IS A NEW SERIES OF 1-HOUR READS WRITTEN BY WORLD-RENOWNED EXPERTS!

These captivating books will help you become the best version of yourself, allowing for new opportunities in your personal and professional life. Accelerate your career and expand your knowledge with these powerful books written on today's hottest ideas.

TRENDING BUSINESS AND PERSONAL GROWTH TOPICS

Read in an hour or less

Leading experts and authors

Bold design and captivating content